AF254851

WATER'S EYE

Photographs
GALEN GARWOOD

Poems
PETER WELTNER

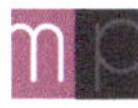

Marrowstone Press, Seattle

for
Robert Mohr

PW

WATER'S EYE

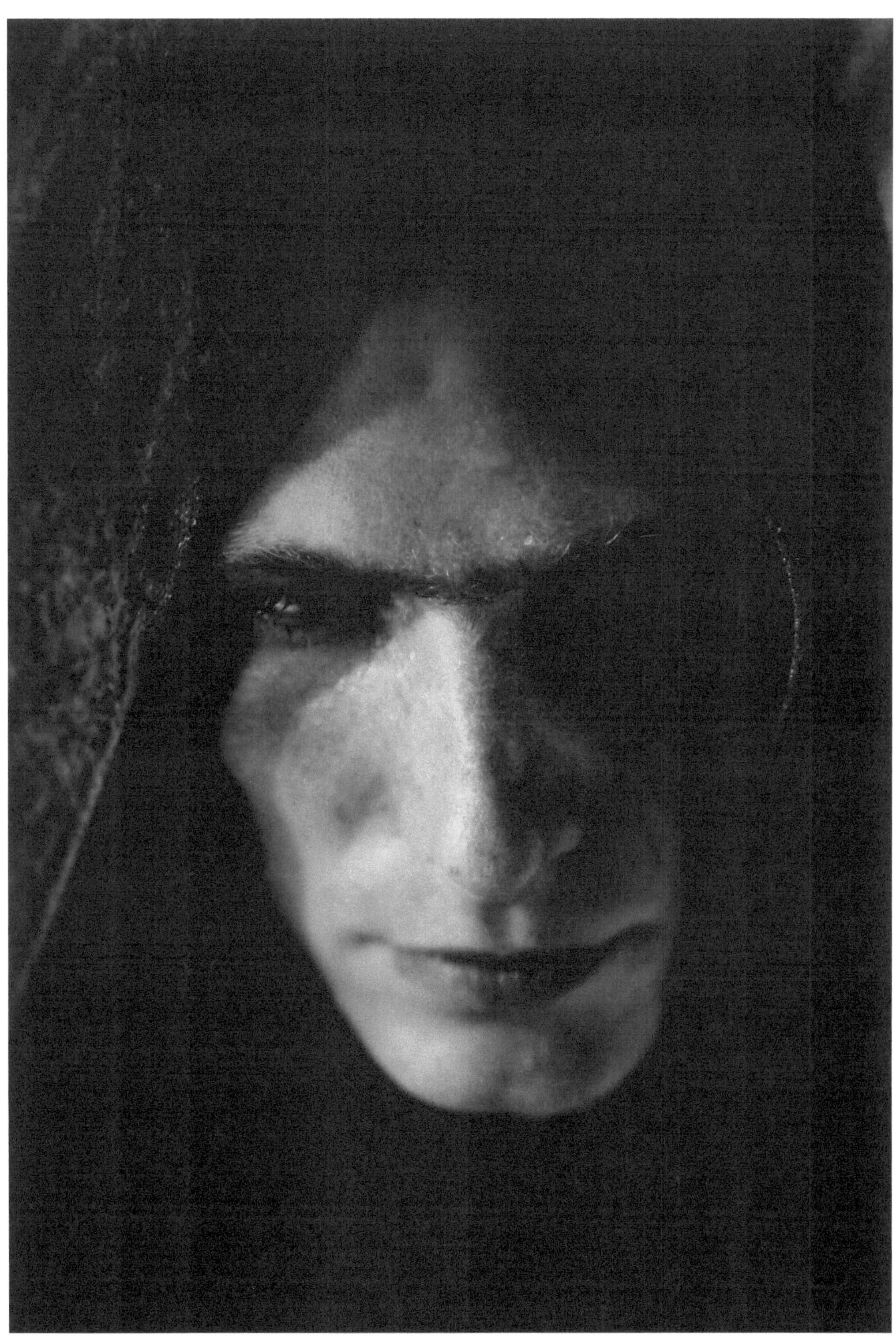

I. Seer

1.

Oracle of the everyday,
seer of the ordinary,
vessel of estrangement,
a face in a photograph stark in its repose,
obscure, a beauty that darkness exposes.
The severity of the magical,
a face like a mask carved from stone,
high, fine cheek bones,
Greco-Roman nose, sharply angled,
noble, shadowed, grimy,
as if soiled with dust or dirt inside the cave
from which he's just emerged to speak.

Not meaning to warn petitioners away,
but cloaked in night,
surrounded by it, eyes closed,
yet lit, piercing,
like a magus deep in meditation,
his soul inspired by
the demons inside him,
the furies that inhabit the world.
What does he see? A history of fear.
A boy watching matinees
and ancient things and midnight shows.
You. Me.

2.

Munchkins, witches, frog green skin,
penknife noses, hothouse chemical flowers,
yellow brick roads, shrunken-man monkey faces,
span of life decided by an hour glass,
peaked hats, broomstick,
wickedness water-wasted,
a color world scarier than black and white,
though, the lord knows, Kansas is bleak—
hard work, dirt, dust, rent overdue,
one streak of bad luck after another,
the richest landowner a bitch,
mean, cheap, a dog- and kid-hater.

What youth's bad dreams are made of,
like the embryos pickled in jars
I saw at a county fair, wrinkled faces,
dung-colored flesh, toes and fingers like claws,
noses never to breathe air. Like Oz. Like Life.
Artificial. Movie-garish. Plastic.
A tornado tonight might whirl me back
into sick, hot wizard colors, portcullis doors,
nightmare magic or leave me
in the swirling funnel in between worlds,
neither this nor that,
lost in a twister, its deafening roar.

3.

Warriors sheet-covered like the Ku Klux Klan,
denizens of an antediluvian underground city.
A lineage like spacemen's. Robots.
A plan to rule the world. Ray guns.
The cruel complicity of Thunder Riders.
Radium powers. Pistol shots. Long elevator tubes.
It's Mu, ruled by Queen Tika,
deposed by outsiders,
the toll of her wickedness,
undone by American cowboys
schooled in the ways of the West,
its mythic power to console.

Saturdays I watch the serial
before I mow my father's lawn and trim the trees.
Job done, I play by the lake until the light dims.
It's noon's sun that worries me most.
What hides under my feet, deep down?
Rock slabs, water, the fiery core of Mu destroyed.
The grass cut clean as a putting green
conceals a void below the earth,
the aftermath of the violence inside,
the shock I feel as I hear
the ground under me speak,
no longer able to keep its silence.

4.

Huge, basalt heads,
gouged, pitted, split,
some decapitated.
Snarling lips, babies' faces
distorted by rage,
stone chips, votive axes,
traces left in caves, in tombs,
figures of jaguars, dumb-struck masks
carved from jadeite, undeciphered X's
like messengers from Mars
in a stone stele, a child, light in weight as an infant,
pliable as wax is, though carved from wood.

An Olmec world that some day
will revive from where it died.
Charms. Chants. Hexes.
I take it all in
as if it were a movie.
No scholar's facts printed on walls,
no inscriptions of songs.
But thoughts of taking blood
someone longs to shed,
a need, a con of a film
I roll in my head
to help me believe this is real, no one's faking.

A dread that never ends
is mine for the taking,

an ancient, collapsed world,
its ruins risen or rising
like zombies from graves,
from earth's prison.
And beautiful,
all of it, every piece,
object, frame I see,
no matter how cruel,
each exceedingly beautiful
and wise.

5.
The brisk wind's crisp,
the air midnight clear,
rich with the smell of things
shifting to winter.
A gull's wing's feathers
lie on the sidewalk
near a trench
being dug for sewer pipes.
The perimeter of the park is edged by hedges.
A man wearing clothes
older than he is
snores on a bench.

A fishing boat, returning late with its haul,
is mooring in its slip.
A cruise ship, waiting on the bay,
shows its colors,

its lights glittering
on the choppy water.
At the curb, a man in a greatcoat
hails a taxi, its tail lights flaming red.
A bleaker sky smothers the moon.
What is there left to see? The night's
a man, face blackened with pitch.

A chill rain falls. A flock of ravens bothers a pole.
A styrofoam cup buried in a ditch
is trying to float. Already so strange in youth,
in old age the world becomes far harder
to read, the truth of it more elusive,
more nightmarish,
like a bridge I must cross,
trying not to panic as my shoes,
coat, hat are getting soaked, of no use in such weather,
no way to escape from the torrent the storm is,
what lurks under earth, below pavement,
its illegible signals and signs.

6.
Like an old man's late in the evening,
a face in a photograph
dreams of something
more real than day, that,
entering sleep, wakens to death,
curious about the dead,
who, denied everything,
desire all. A face that midnight imitates,
of a man still young, his beauty so real

it can't help but be cruel, as time is
when it makes a man
take his last breath.

He leaves this world for some other,
with the face of a man of grave pleasures
to whom the mysteries of caves,
their well guarded secrets,
what's hidden underground,
have been revealed by phallus and loins.
The cold nocturnal face, near despair,
of passion, of ecstasy,
a seer's rapture
saved from oblivion
by the lens of a camera,
refracted by water's watchful eyes.

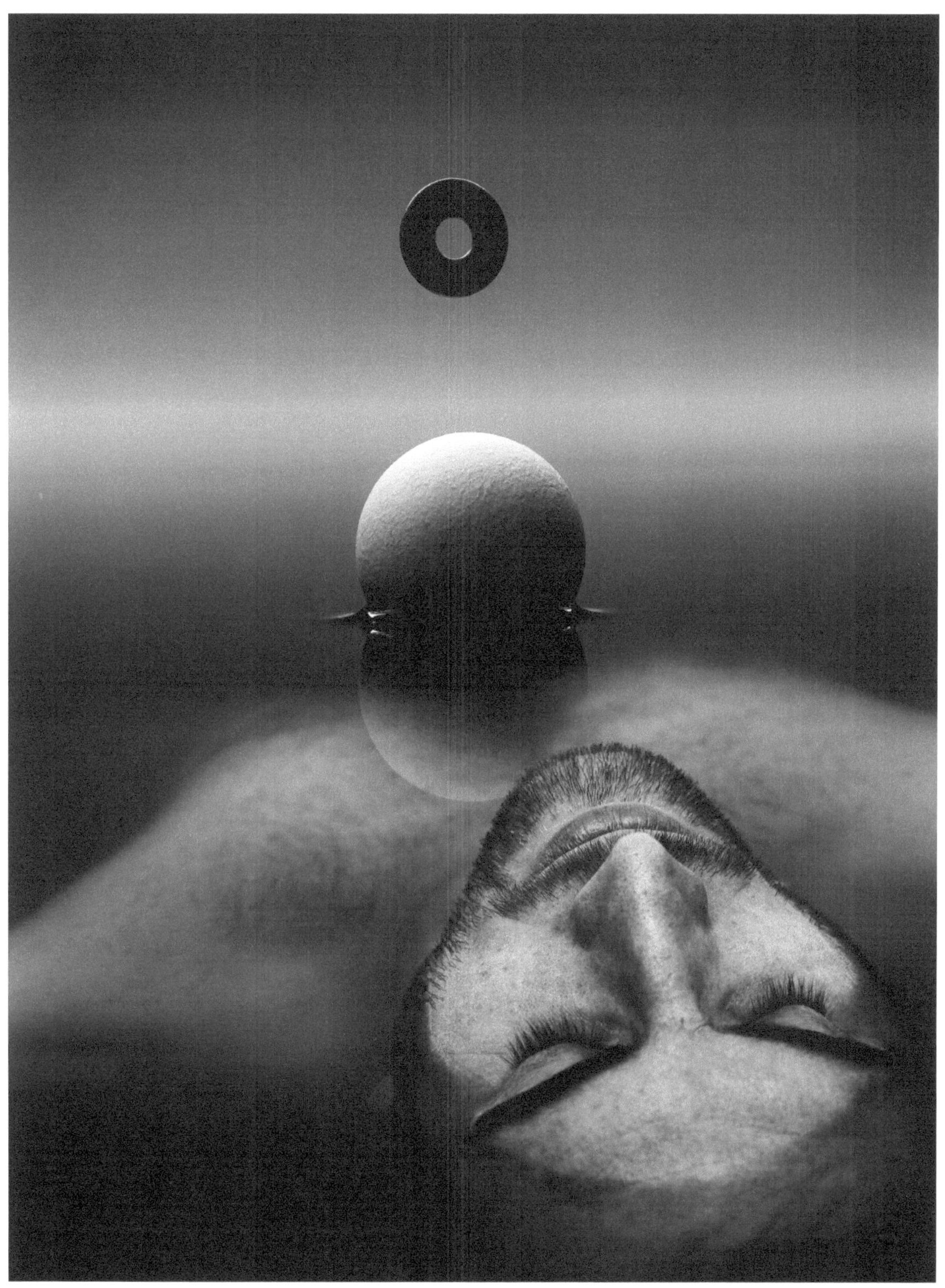

II. A Poem Beginning with a Man Floating in Water

1.

As stones or pebbles below the surface
desire, would seek the freedom of air,
a man longs to be water. His body floats dreamily,
sky and lake one, undivided,
the slim horizon blurred, smudged gray.

A half-lit sphere floats too,
a lunar dream, perhaps, as the light
and shadows of his reveries loom
over the lake. His flesh reflects the moon,
its watery double easy to see through.

Suspended in air, a hole cut out of it,
rimmed by light, a carved circular stone,
is dark as the man's black eyebrows and beard.

Say a man sleeping in a lake
dreams of a ring, some perfectly made thing
unfound in nature, what only a mind and hands
can create. Say it is an image of itself
that his body most needs, that he often dreams of.

A rock transformed into a stony amulet
hangs in the sky, a talismanic guide
to what living means, the circle of light and dark,

globe and ring, the order of things drowned in water
like a snake taken by the sea, an engulfed island or cathedral.
May a man's body be buoyed up by the deep,
unsinking in peace, undrowning in a lake as he dreams
of a paradisal calm, of a sea's timelessness.

2.
He comes in disguise, like emptiness,
like the void heard in unsaid goodbyes.
The day's fogged-in. I can barely see
three feet ahead unless I'm wrong
and it's night when he enters my room.

He's a guy in black jeans and scruffy black beard
or a ghost, a phantom I can believe in
if I'm sleepy enough. His face is on the wall.
When I feel lost, I concentrate on it or on his black jeans.
On the floor, by the foot of my bed, I hear weeping.

Then I see her head, her haunches, her right rear paw.
I tickle behind her ear. She used to like that.
There's a wind sifting through trees.
It makes a crackling sound to remind me
how she didn't like the sand blowing in her eyes

or the shifting ground under her feet
while we walked on dunes. I hear my own crying
as if it were someone else's, my father's.

I remember his defying death, outlasting his diseases,
a stone in a raging creek until they washed him away
into the water he'd been since before he was born.

3.
All mourning aspires to constancy.
Refusing to be comforted, it claims a life's
a Greek ship's stern, a plow that breaks
the sea like earth. I've read that somewhere.
Or watched it on clips from a movie.

Refugees, exiled at birth, tell tall tales
to pass the time. My mother's grief
won't mean anything when
there's no one left to recall it. Without brothers,
I walk in nothing, in air, in clearest air.
"It's time," my mother said, and died.
The way of paradise is unrenewable
and never lies. The meadow I live near
demands I obey it, says,
"Go home to where you were born."

I refuse to leave here. Despair is too enticing,
a tail biting snake that must devour itself
to survive. I wonder who's seducing whom.
My mother said a dream is a creek that runs
through a wide green field, gathering tears

until it becomes a stream, a river
and flows, all sorrow repealed,
into the sea, *mare*, timelessness, *agape*.

4.
It's raining, good weather for disbelieving in reality.
Dense thickets in woods, mist steaming from a waterfall.
It's my last summer. Childhood's over.
I reek of sod, oak roots, needles, brush.
A pool. A cascading creek cut from rock.

I've lost my time for endless play. Rhododendron petals
swirl in the froth. I left my bike at the trail head.
Zigzag twists over the pass,
then a long hike to where I can ride it again,
the long trip home, the unsafe roads and highway.

I remember this thirty years later. Robert smells good,
like pine. I beg him wait to wash off
his sweaty skin. It tastes like resin would,
his body as wild as faraway woods.
Sometimes a loss is forgotten until it returns like a lover.

I'm caught by the half-light in the pine forest
around my lake. I want dreams to stay,
to keep singing strangely. I want water to mean everything.

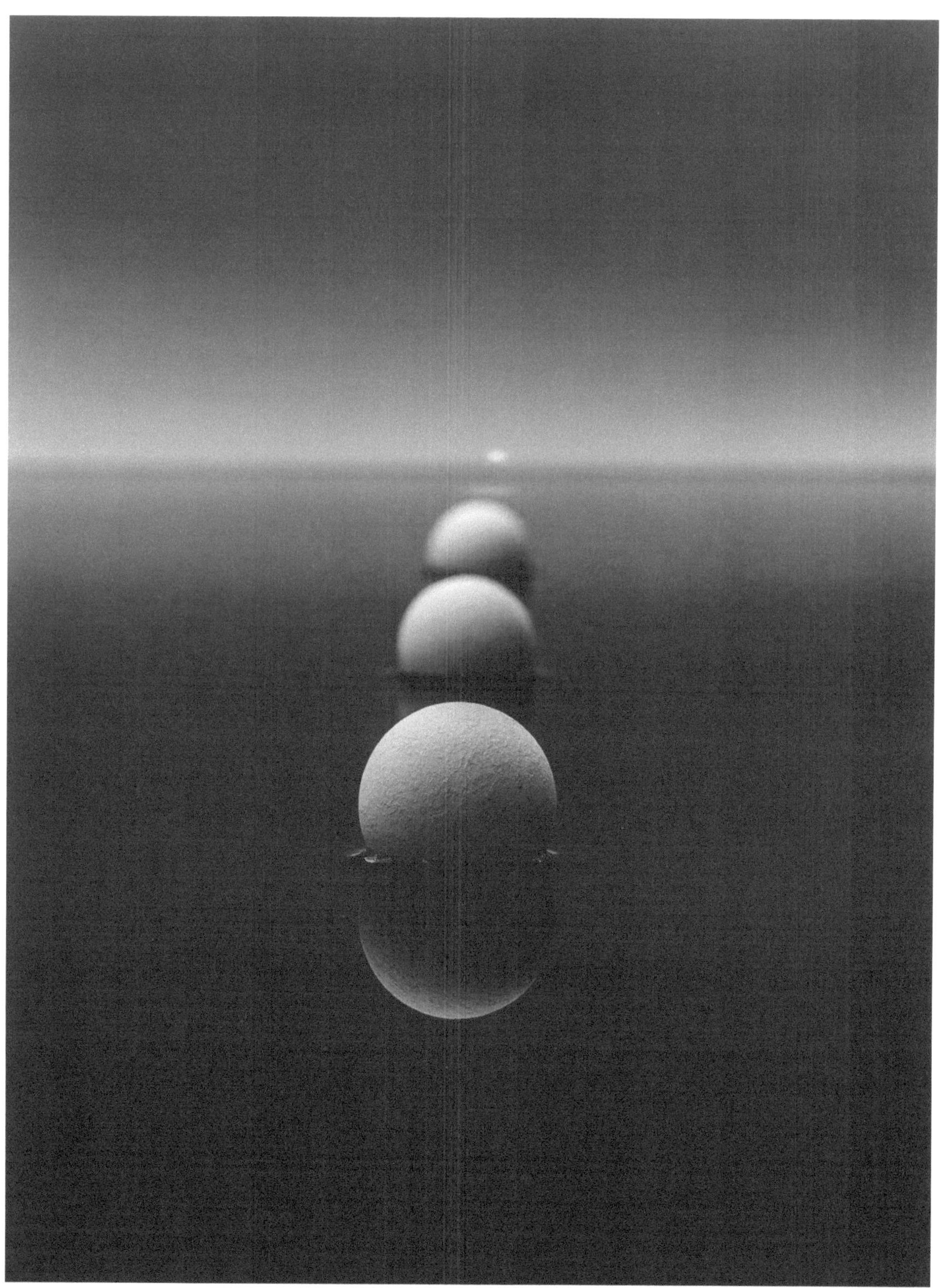

III. Memory Setting

1.

Not a woman, she is the body he's lost,
the man I'll call O, in the meadow
he'd been strolling through
composing a song in his mind,
oblivious of his plight, the flight below the earth
where his love has gone
where it doesn't belong
among the shades.

He'd been preoccupied by
the beauty of the scene,
the flowers, the clear sky, the generous grass
until he was riven, sundered in two,
no longer able to love, who knows why.
Call it Death's fault.
All music mourns.
But on this day his grieving begins.

It was his flesh that had given him his art.
Without it, or sex, a man is a specter.
The way down is perilous, led only by a hope,
a story he tells himself
that lights the scarily steep ledge
and frightens the furies inside him
who would keep him from himself,
his ravaged body.

He's being tried, with no time for juries
or a lawyer's exhortations,
and sings the tune alone stones listen to,

the longing they recall to him.
To humanity, I mean, never to change.
And O, this man who is nothing,
who is dead without love,
in your sad songs
they can hear Death coming
to return your heart to you.
And you happily take it inside you
only to look back
too passionately
and lose it again.

Remember your loss
is why we remember you.

2.

After my mother died
in a blank, bleakly white
hospital room,
her face contorted
in a postmortem fright mask,
I dreamed
of her alive every night for weeks,
for months.

As I've dreamed much longer of him,
my father, beginning on the day
he slipped away
from one sleep to another.
As I dream of so many I've loved,
dead from the plague
or like sweet Jay
killed by a dread disease.

But I also often see them
while I'm completely awake,
in a sort of vision. Ghosts, I suppose.
I don't know. Maybe it is only memory,
playing its magic tricks on me,
no matter the reason
or the mood I'm in.
What does it mean to be truly dead?
Is it to be forgotten? I can see them speak,
I can hear what they say or sing to me,
but they are not real. Who, once the sun is shining,
or in a hard rain, with its own moment's fantasies,
truly remembers yesterday's dreams?
And this, this light of you I see
sneaking into my room,
is my reality, the start of my new day.

3.
The angry heat of sun at noon.
A slow, long hike like the ones he took with Ishmael,
two lonely boys, he much stronger than Isaac.
When Isaac looks for him now,
his eyes search behind lost years to the desert
where his half brother and Ishmael's mother
heard the cries of jackals at night.
Their fears are his still.

He hears, sees—as if he were the brother
his father's exiled to nowhere,
lost, a wanderer,
to be no one, where water's unknown—
knows the cruel, bold boast his old father will make.
"God's will be done." Isaac carries the twigs

and tree limbs only for the sake
of his hearing him lie to him.
They climb the rims of hills,
reach a thicket,
brambles, bushes, weeds, a clearing by it,
where it starts, the sickness unto death,
human misery. He stops,
sits on rocks,
slips the faggots off his back meant for sacrifice,
for the pyre.

Now his father is lagging behind him,
sent by God with knife and fire, he says.
But he's unable to do it
and drops the knife. The ram is mythology,
a fable, the tale Abraham
has the wit to tell his wife: what Jahweh
wanted him to kill
instead of his son.

At his death-bed, who will bear
the sacrificial knife?
And Isaac repeats the same story,
tells the same lies
about an angel and a ram,
his father released
from God's command,
Isaac the boy,

a child, who saw on Moriah's ground
in an endless horizon
the millions death bound,
sacrificed on altars like his
on that day he'd have given all,

even his life, if only history
would deny he'd ever lived,
that any God had demanded death of them.

4.
I traveled back to Filbert Street last night,
where it's always empty and dark.
I moved out twenty five years ago. Torn down,
it's merely a barren lot
that nothing can be done about,
too costly to develop. I must be circumspect, quiet.
I don't want the landlords
to suspect I'm here.

For years, I've quit paying rent.
The threat of discovery scares me.
Both bridges' lights are barely visible in the fog.
I find things I've left behind,
a record player, a few LPs,
a rubber tree, a zebra shade,
stuff I've had to take by stealth
since memory's a thief.

I try the shower. The water stays hot.
On a cabinet door, there's the old cleft mark
left by a long lost screw driver.
The pilot light's on. The refrigerator works.
The toilets run. I'm almost young again,
not locked in age,
anticipating those I've bedded here
until morning appears.

I've heard time is a page in a book you turn.
It isn't. The walls need re-painting,
the carpets a good cleaning.
At Coit Tower, the usual party goes on.
My upstairs neighbor sings erotic duets
with her German boyfriend,
the banger, bald and ardent.
I listen, attune to their mattress springs.

One day I watched my possessions
hauled away. Yet some I cling to linger here,
there, in a bedroom where I cannot sleep
from fear of death, like a caress by a hand
I still feel on my face, recall night after night
as if I'm asleep, though I can't remember his name,
just his kisses before they disappeared,
prolonged, anonymous, and tender.

5.

The sun sets over water
as flat and black as the Salton Sea.
Three suns sit in the water
black and flat as the Salton Sea.
All poetry is repetition.
Look how the surface mirrors
each one as if it were a crescent moon,
the light the earth turns into shadow.

A triad of globes floats
on the buoyant
lake water, each one brighter
than the distant sun,
unmoving, yet seeming

to be reaching closer
to the real sun each
is seeking to become.

Or the memory of it, the light that sets,
that will soon disappear,
the world cast back to darkness
unless these three suns stay
unspinning where they are,
their light as cold as moons',
lasting past the night
floating on glassy water.

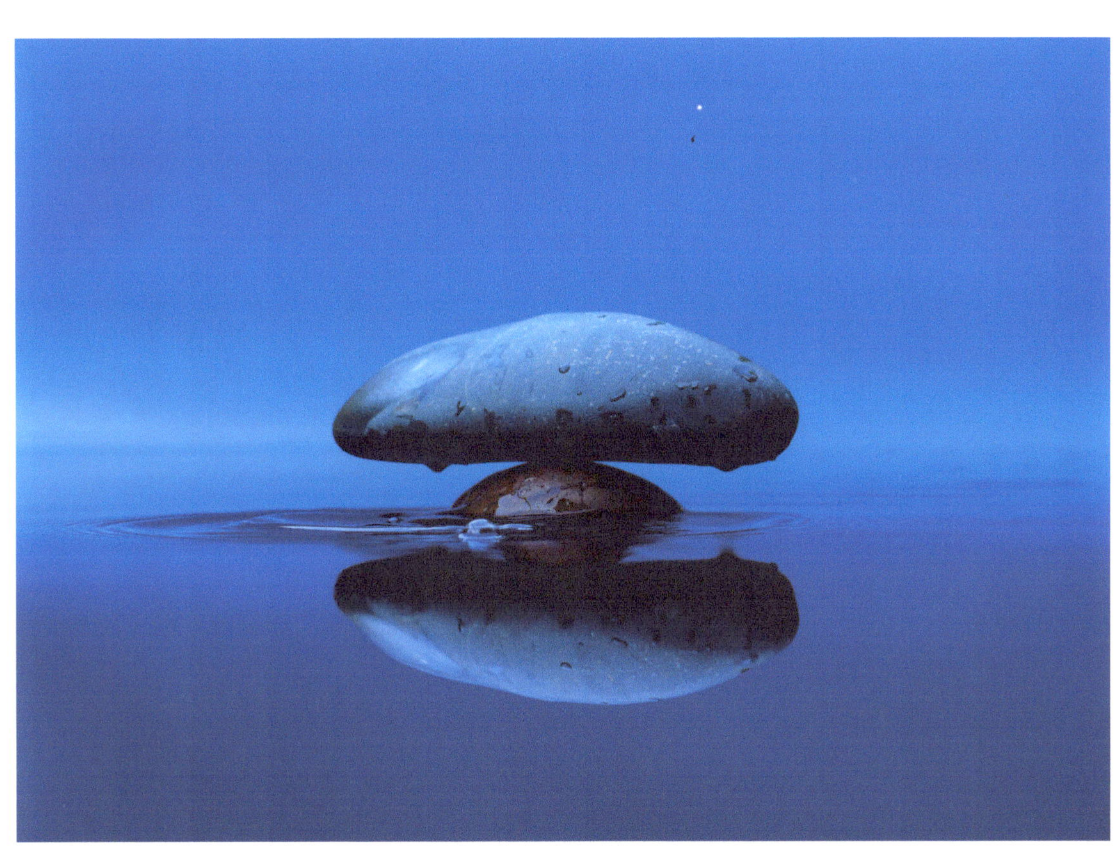

IV. Stones

1.

A man flees from his homeland into exile,
seeking safety in France.
Deutschland allows his kind no more.
The war starts. Paris falls—
he should have believed it would happen—
into enemy hands.

He's sitting in a *taberna,*
sipping a whiskey
near the Pyrenees.
He has no visa, no passport,
trapped, the border closed,
all routes by sea denied him.

How could he have hoped
he might find freedom?
It's past midnight. The barkeep
has long gone to bed.
The shutters and doors are locked.
There's no way to be saved, ahead or back.

He smells a suckling pig
being roasted on an open spit.
He dreams that night of a stone,
casting no shadow, baking in the Spanish sun
above an unmarked grave,
or washed in its waves by the Bay of Biscay.

2.

A woman in a downpour before dawn
helplessly wanders
the southbound lanes of The Great Highway,

mumbling to herself
or crying out into the dark something unspeakable
or raving in despair,

"Friends, friends," to the air,
to the rain-veiled streetlights.
Driving too fast, cars swerve,
trying not to hit her.
She's heavy set, her clothes
a stormy night's pickings from a garbage dump.

The ocean's screaming back at her.
She hollers louder at the waves
mocking her. She pretends to the winds
to be singing,
though phlegm chokes her voice.
As the tempest moves east,

the moon peeks through a gold ring.
Deeper water is luring her in.
The scattered stars mean nothing.
She's becoming the shells
and the bones
that the sand under her feet

once belonged to,
the beach no one knows,
the grit between her toes,
a stone
a child picks up
and throws into the ocean.

3.
He feels anonymous, a gravestone
in the cemetery in back of the library,
names and dates moss covered,

weather-worn, unreadable
like a book with many torn
or lost pages.

Its gothic brick façade is fated
to be demolished, the empty lot sold,
its flagstone walkway jackhammered
into gravel, the dead spots in the grass
after the last slab, dark as the silhouettes
or shadows in a late Jasper Johns.

He saves a chunk, small as a pebble
from a broken headstone he'll store
on a shelf for the past's sake,
like stories memory keeps
minerally quiet or the stillness
of ripples at night in a lake.

4.
A large ovoid stone, a skull,
beaked, bird eyed, eagle gray,
spotted, partially wet, dripping,
lies delicately balanced on a smaller rock,
red brown, indented,
ridged like a cranium,

an exposed brain
that's mostly submerged in water
though supported by the shimmering
reflection of the bird's skull
that reclines on it. Concentric circles,
ripples ceremoniously surround the two,

as if they were bound together,
enclosing, expanding an infinite view
of an all blue world,
the blue of shot silk
or Nicholas Poussin
or even Yves Klein.

There's a single star, a pin point,
a prick, a tiny white hole in the sky, no other illumination,
the sky, water become one,
lit from within as blue is lit by the blue inside it,
the mind a distant, barely visible light,
one dreaming stone resting precariously atop another.

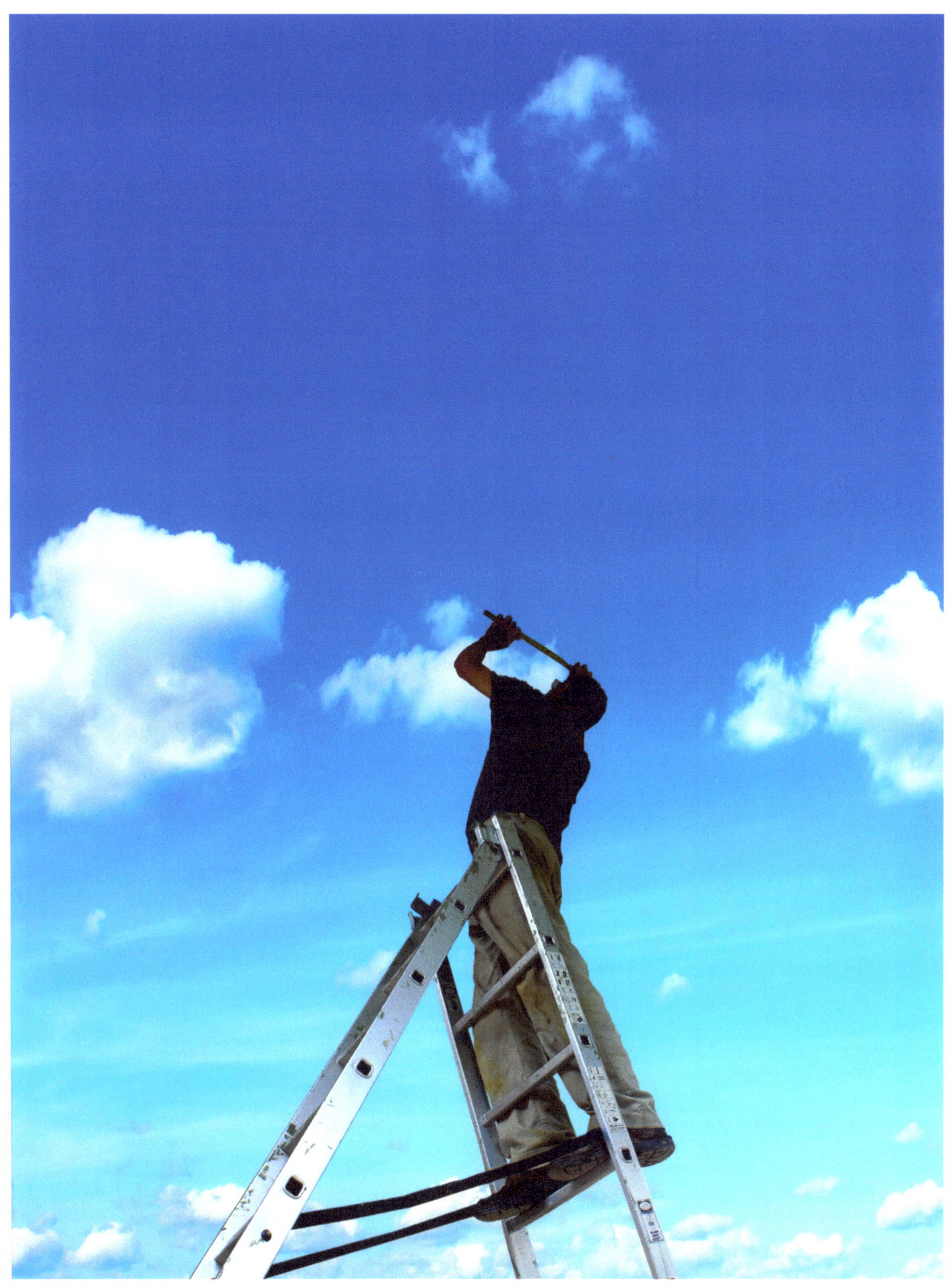

V. Ladders

1.

With both hands he holds a stick
or some tool for measurement
or one more, smaller rung
he would climb if he could
of the ladder he stands on,
two steps from the last.
It's a laborer's ladder,
functional, used, unbeautiful.
He's wearing workman's pants, paint splattered,
and old fashioned laborer's shoes.

The imagination begins in practicality.
Suppose what he sees
when he stares up at the sky,
gazes high up into a dark blue
that lightens as it nears the horizon,
streaked with thin, gauzy ribbons of cirrus clouds,
a flock of cumulus drifting past;
suppose the sky he is trying to gauge,
the heavens he's trying to measure
belong not, as it seems, to day but to night.

The lone star that shines's not the last one remaining
from yesterday's dark
but the first one in this strange evening's noon-bright sky.
What if this is what night looks like in paradise.

What if this is Jacob's ladder he stands on,
so curiously ordinary, easy to find in any workman's garage
or shed, and he, like Jacob,
is doomed to wrestle with an angel with the strength of a god
and to beat him, he who is now standing on his ladder
searching for where the angel's gone, too far away to see.

2.
The world is sometimes lost in sorrow,
overwhelmed by the power of it.
In the Philippines, a child vanishes,
washed out to sea.
The tortured in Lhasa or Guantanamo
are left to trick themselves into sleep in their rooms.
What use are images of atrocity in the news?
Too much is made of magnitude

when the silence of pain may be heard in the everyday,
in a neighbor wounded in bootcamp

who's awake all night, all day cleans his guns,
the widow who dresses in smocks
and peeks through her shabby lace curtains,
the grandmother who makes faces at her grandson,
tugging at his snotty sleeve,
the dull-eyed cult member who roams the neighborhood,
his windows littered with decaying food,
the imaginary ladder he appears always to be climbing,
grasping invisible rung after rung, trying to reach
whatever above him he fervently needs.

3.

In Kure Beach, I'm walking on a spit of land,
past splintered posts, broken shutters,
flattened dunes, the ever changing waters
off the coast. If it's our dread of death
that makes the world holy,
then the world is holy.
Tides are breaking free over rocks,
tugging shell shards and driftwood
back into natural sluices,
washing the sand

where loggerhead turtles lay their eggs,
food for ghost crabs.
Ungainly pelicans take off from the beach
so beautifully it catches my breath.
It's an Eden of laurel oak and live oak,
sweet smelling bay, hornbeam, ironwood,
flowering dogwood, red azalea
that forest the back hill ridges,
the wetland swales.
Beyond the dunes,

red maple, cedar, black pine, marsh grasses,
cattails, rivulets, deer, wild goats, and musk
hide in noon-thin shadows.
The warblers are returning
before the hawks and raptors.
Green bushes and leaves
and ferns, it's spring, renewing the world,
that hurts me most when faith is gone,

a love, like most loves,
abruptly, swiftly wounding whenever it's lost.

Here on the Carolina coast
I once saw the sun rise in the west
or set in the east, an illusion of tides,
a scant moment when all seemed reversed,
upended, as he and I,
two boys together just for a while,
under the sun, in the dunes,
easily climbed an old oak as if its low hanging limbs
were steps on a ladder to see what we thought
we'd be able to see, uncannily, much better there.

4.
The streets are as silent as the sky.
A desert heat blankets the ocean.
The beach quietly cowers.
The fence below my room
is shaking from a hungry raccoon
who surmounts it in search of food
as easily as a ladder.
I hear leaves
rustling in the park, dew-wet,
dripping, the trails still too slick

to walk on this early,
dawn at least an hour away,
and two girls' laughter,
their hearts set
on the beach,
where they'll wait patiently

for the sun's reflection in the sea,
calm as a lake this morning,
as the light begins
from behind the hills its effortless climb.

5.
The magnanimity of blue,
of all it belongs to,
painterly blues–
prussian, cerulean, cobalt, ultramarine–
the unseen peace,
munificence,
it seems to imply,
water as sky,
earth as air,
the elements as paradise.

The way up is the way down.
Death's the blue flame
of the everyday
that burns a ladder's wood away
or the ordinary rain that rusts it,
leaving nothing more to climb on,
no tools you can or need to use,
leaving the sky eternally blue,
blue as the pure land's
prayed for gracious sky or sea is.

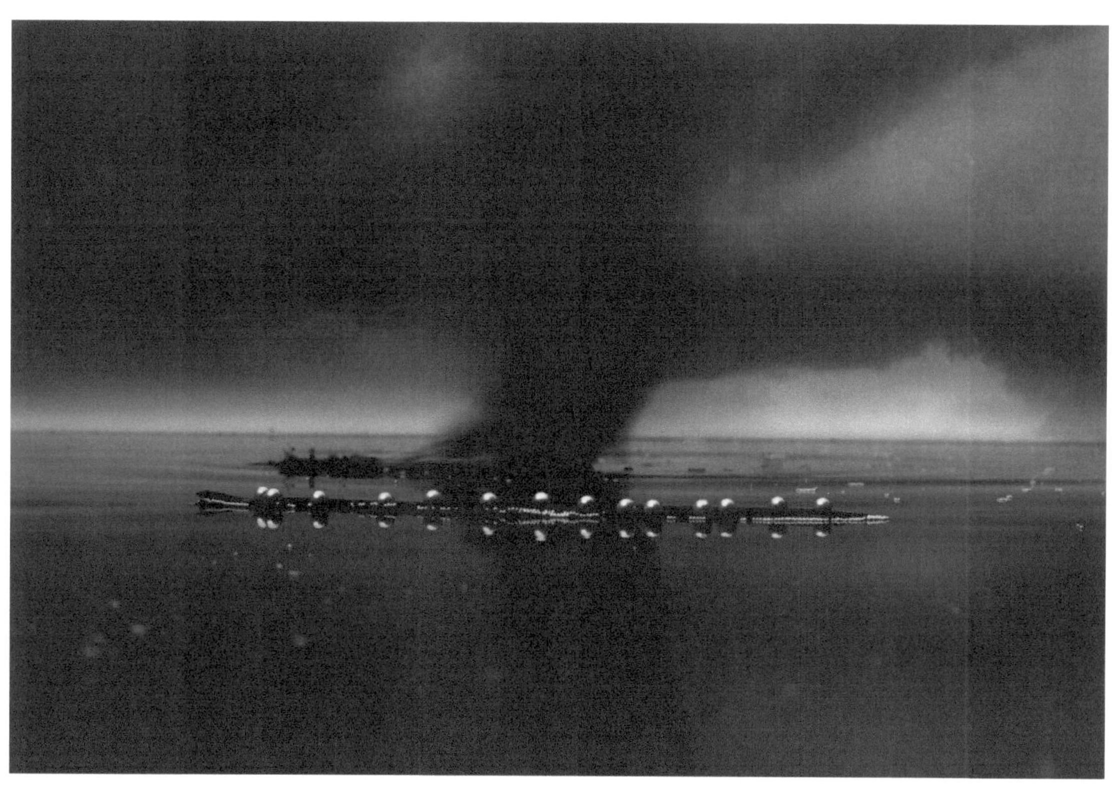

VI. The Storm Chosen

1.

The sea's is the way of memory.
It's the first day of fall,
the inception of the skeletal season,
of stripping away,
of things beginning their decay.

I'm trying to learn
what not to be means
in this changing weather,
in the shifting waves,
the stir in the air of cooler breezes.

My young dog and I
climb the dunes and spy on
two lovers embracing,
sleeping beneath a sky
whose azure's deeper than the ocean's.

The brightly surging tide
almost reaches their blankets
in the lair they have dug
for themselves
between sea grass and sand.

Shells' smells delight my dog
and me as I watch him sniff.
All there is to know is what each wave
roars in to tell me,
anonymity,

like a well which,
when I shout "Peter"
into it, echoes
my name
in dying reverberations.

Perhaps the last thing I'll glimpse
will be an albatross
or more likely a pelican,
its wings tipped by dawn
as it glides toward the sun,

or the scruffy gull
I watched earlier this morning
as it swooped and soared and played in the wind
before it glided north on its currents
toward the black cliffs of the headlands.

2.
I dream through each day,
no matter the time,
reading a book, listening to music,
re-enacting my life, looking for the rhyme
that ties past to present,

a storm at sea
in a ring of pearls.
Say this island is somewhere
in the Mediterranean
or in the Caribbean,

far off Cuba's coast,
where sins are purged,
Prospero's isle
of strange voices and sweet music
and charms,

and a tempest's
at ease amidst its rage,
and battered sailors pray
for the winds to blow
but not so strongly,

for the waves to rise,
high enough to sail on
but no higher, for the voyage
to be graced with fair skies.
And I, that I be forgiven.

3.
When I die, let me be the sea,
profound, deep, ebb tide or neap,
my fate god-willed,
currents unstilled. Let me be
the sea,

be its brother, the earth my mother
my father the form of it,
island and storm.
Let me be the sea,
its waters

the daughters of mercy,
be forgiven again and again,
windward or lee. Let me be the sea,
not weary,
but free, no more fear,
spared more being
hurled from year to year.
Let me be the sea, my journey

an endless day, the way home,
atoned, come by sea to be saved,
redeemed, dreamed of
by a lover
from a long ago world.

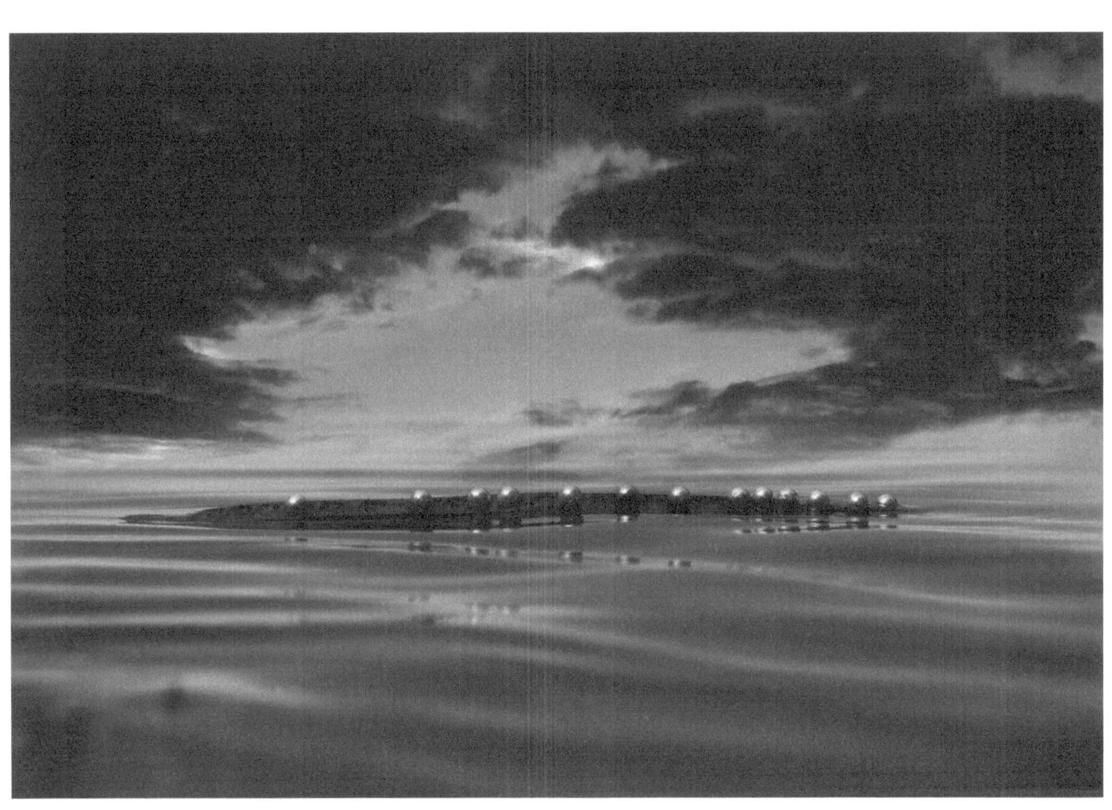

Peter Weltner has published five books of fiction, three poetry chapbooks, three collaborations with Galen Garwood, and four full length books of poetry, most recently *To the Final Cinder* and *Stone Altars*, both from BrickHouse Books. He lives near the Pacific with his husband, Atticus Carr.

Galen Garwood has collaborated with a number of poets including Sam Hamill, *Passport*, 1989, *Mandala*, 1993, William O'Daly, *The Road to Isla Negra*, 2015, and three books with Peter Weltner, *Water's Eye*, 2015, *Where Everything Is Water As Far As He Can See*, 2012, and *The One-Winged Body*, 2011. He lives and makes art in a small village in Northern Thailand.

Notes on the Photographs

page 1   *Portrait of John*, Savannah, Georgia, 1995

page 8   *Remembrance*, 'the Dream Sea,' Thailand, 2015

page 14   *Akalixy Totem*, 'the Dream Sea,' Thailand, 2015

page 22   *Sleeping Stone, Breathing Star*, 'the Dream Sea,' Thailand, 2015

page 28   *Self-Portrait*, Thailand, 2014

page 34   *Pearls of Shiva*, 'the Dream Sea,' Thailand, 2015

page 39   *Raft of Pearls*, 'the Dream Sea,' Thailand, 2015